LIVABLE LUXE

BRIGETTE ROMANEK

CHRONICLE CHROMA

To my girls, Willow and Isobel, you are everything.

To my ride or dies, Missy and Gwyneth, this journey
is made better by you ladies. Thank you.

Nareg, my Nareg, thank you for hanging in there with
me. Brings me joy to work with you every day.

My mama, my hero. Your courage, strength,
kindness, curiosity, support, and creativity inspire
me every day. I love you so very much.

FOREWORD

by Gwyneth Paltrow

Brigette and I met in the late winter of 2000, a particularly grey winter to my memory. I was filming the now epochal film, *The Royal Tenenbaums*, up in the striking New York City neighborhood of Hamilton Heights—unfamiliar to me, even though I had grown up a mere three miles away. Every day I would travel from the heart of the West Village up to the gorgeous, imposing house, don my wig and kohl black eyeliner, and immerse myself in the world that Wes Anderson was creating. I loved that job, but it came at a particularly lonely time in my life. I felt unmoored, like I wasn't quite sure of my direction; maybe I was questioning my calling.

Brigette came to visit the set one day, and I was drawn to her: her beauty, her warmth, her authenticity. Sometimes in life you meet someone and think, "We are going to be friends." And that is exactly what transpired. At the time, Brigette was a singer who had a beautiful voice and a promising career ahead of her. When we spoke about it, I recognized a reticence in her voice. She said she felt a shyness that she thought might not behoove her; was she questioning her calling?

During the ensuing years, Brigette and I were like two propagating waves of the same type, intersecting and fluctuating as we went on journeys to explore what our callings might reveal themselves to be. We were expats in London together, eating Thanksgiving dinner at our house in Belsize Park, going to the Frieze art fair (before it became global), being each other's wingmen at various events. Brigette and I gravitated toward the same things—great art, real friendship, great food—and our kids played together in the garden (while we had the occasional glass of wine). We loved the things that made us feel whole and inspired, the art and architecture of London, our little kids, and the idea of possibility. I started to orient around an idea that would use the internet to connect people to meaningful things. She started orienting around an idea that would bring meaning to people in the way they lived.

She started slowly, doing her own house first, helping a friend or two in the process. And then one day it was crystal clear—her calling had found her.

The spaces that Brigette designs are extraordinary. She has the most unique eye and is able to create the most original, unexpected spaces. It's like she can feel what the room is calling out to be and then will manifest it. She will spend hours finding just the right light, the exquisite chair you never would have thought of. In the three projects we have now done together, she pushed my design boundaries and excited me with a new way of seeing things. All while making our spaces feel like they are places to love and be loved in. I am drawn to her spaces for the same reasons I was drawn to her all those years ago: the beauty, the warmth, and the authenticity.

—Gwyneth Paltrow

INTRODUCTION

by Brigette Romanek

My grandmother worked at RR Donnelley Printing. It was a factory that produced magazines and catalogs. She'd come home at midnight, six nights a week, and throw some of those magazines and catalogs on the kitchen table for anyone to look at. The only one to care—was me.

Turning the pages was a view into different worlds, people, and locations. New environments, styles, and interesting images. Rooms that had walls painted in different colors—not just white—or even, possibly, wallpaper! Unusual pieces of furniture, not just the one style I knew. Amazing landscapes . . . I could go on. In other words, the way others existed.

I am proud to have grown up on the South Side of Chicago. These magazines were just a way to see there was more out there. I know now that they were mostly staged photographs, but I wouldn't have cared, because I still got to see new and interesting things I'd never seen before that weren't part of my world.

Then, there was, and still is, my mama. A single mom. A rock and roller through and through, radiating such infectious energy and style. When she was growing up, she was the one that was "different" to her siblings. My aunts are nurses and teachers, and my uncle, a preacher. My mom knew she wanted to see the world and be a singer. She had that carefree rebel spirit about her. She believed in living life to the fullest and making your own rules. We had apartments where she had friends paint murals on our living room walls, or she'd paint a room purple if she felt it, and then paint it green the next day! She had an unusually large, wood, four-poster bed built, with stairs, because it was so high. I'd come home from school, and she'd say, "We're moving!" That might mean a different house—or state. I changed schools like most people change their socks.

Grandma Doris

She traveled the world through her singing. That gave her an open mind and way of thinking about the world. She traveled and sang with Marvin Gaye, David Bowie, Michael Jackson, Bette Midler, Quincy Jones, Mary J. Blige, Sarah Vaughan, Aretha Franklin, and Jennifer Lopez, just to name a few. And when she'd come home, she'd bring me lots of gifts. From unique clothing to objects—items that represented the local cultures: fabrics, dolls, pillows, masks, clothes, blankets, and jewelry. Obviously, I looked forward to her coming home!

My mom being an artist, sometimes we had money, and other times we didn't. It didn't really matter because we knew how to make each place a home, and most importantly the feeling *of* a home. I learned to mix the high-price items with low-price items. I'm grateful that it taught me all the items had value, as long as it had its own story. So, from my magazines, and learning from my mom's taste and free spirit, and acquiring special items from all over the world, I became more and more fearless with each new place. Each a new canvas.

My mom, Paulette McWilliams, and Marvin Gaye.

I'm sad to say that most of the items are long gone through all the moves we made, but the feeling I remember so well. That each piece was something especially for me. That it was different to what anyone else had. That each item had a story, an origin, that was now mine. Even that young, I knew my story was different and unique to anyone else's. Whether it was a big or small object, expensive or just one dollar, it all meant the same to me. Special items that I loved! By the time I was twelve, I had a very eclectic mix of things I'd take from house to house.

While moving states and cities brought new joys, it was also difficult. Always the new kid in school, leaving friends, often the only African American. Sometimes we lived in a beautiful apartment or house, and other times not so beautiful. I was quiet and shy. I didn't share my feelings very much. My mom was my rock. But to handle all the changes, my saving grace was always my space. My room in the house. My respite from all the challenges. After a while I didn't know it but I developed a formula. It wasn't about a style, because we'd move to Spanish or modern houses, sometimes large, sometimes small. But it was always about that feeling in the space. I wanted to make sure I felt at ease, safe, surrounded by items that brought me joy and comfort. I always said to myself, when I was big, and running my own life, I would make my home feel this way. I had no idea this would become the ethos of my design career, creating spaces for people that brought in feeling, an energy, encapsulating memories of their life—a livable luxury.

Something else that has had a great impact on me is understanding the importance of living well. For me, it means living in a place where the most important thing is the ability to exhale, to not worry about items but enjoy them—not living in a precious way. No rooms that are off-limits—I want to enjoy every room and space!

On our final move together, once we'd settled in, my mom told me she was going on a world tour with Luther Vandross. We discussed what should happen with me, and in the end, decided I would stay on my own in California. I was seventeen.

My saving grace was always my space. My room in the house. My respite from all the challenges. After a while I didn't know it, but I developed a formula. It wasn't about a style, because we'd move to Spanish or modern houses, sometimes large, sometimes small. But it was always about that feeling in the space. I wanted to make sure I felt at ease, safe, surrounded by items that brought me joy and comfort.

I always said to myself, when I was big, and running my own life, I would make my home feel this way. I had no idea this would become the ethos of my design career, creating spaces for people that brought in feeling, an energy, encapsulating memories of their life—a livable luxury.

I knew I needed to do something and something fast to make a living. For the next twelve years, I worked in retail stores, started singing, and then designed handbags. But then, I stopped it all to raise my daughters.

The loves of my life.

In 2012, we were living in London, and it was time to move back to Los Angeles. We needed a house, and we needed it quickly, to get the girls ready for the beginning of the school year. The house I found and liked the most, no one in my family liked. But everything I had learned from the way I had lived as a child helped me see the house through a different lens. I told my family I could make that house great.

In six weeks' time, when they walked back into the house they hated before, they all loved it. I created our family home. The house that started my interior design career. It was an organic start. I got my first interior design job from friends just coming over to visit and liking the look and feel of our home.

I never studied design, but I had the school of life that had been teaching me all along. And my mom telling me I could do anything. Believe me, it was hard, but I am grateful. Grateful that I've found my voice, my career love.

If I can share with people the feeling of being in a safe place, a joyous space, a beautiful, memorable space for them, surrounded by things they love, how lucky am I?

All my lessons learned bring me to this . . .

Lots of love,
Brigette

PROJECTS

My look is about eclecticism. Mixing.

It's all about elegance and being classic, while also having a little bit of whimsy and fun.

It doesn't matter what century or decade it's from—if pieces look great together, I have at it.

DON'T GET TOO EXCITED

That was the subject line of the email my husband sent to me.

I will never forget it. Before I opened the email, my mind was swirling. You creatives know what I'm talking about. Was it a film he was going to direct? A gift? A dog?? I didn't know. I prepared myself before opening the email. Remember, my life had been a lot of surprises. I told myself to breathe.

It read: *Rick thinks you should have his Laurel Canyon house.* Mark's good friend, Rick Rubin, owned the Laurel Canyon house that—over the next few years—became a big part of my heart.

Rick hadn't let anyone have the house or do any decorating. He *had* allowed people to live there while recording an album—bands he worked with, or artists that were friends of his. The living room was a recording studio. The house has such an incredible energy and soul; it makes such sense that people would record and feel creative being there. The Red Hot Chili Peppers, Thom Yorke, and it was rumored Jimi Hendrix and even the Beatles graced the house.

And Rick was trusting me. Trusting me to take the house that he had owned since the '90s. He had visited us at the Hancock Park house I revamped, and when he left, he called Mark and kindly said, "Brigette should have the Laurel Canyon house."

I went to meet with Rick over lunch, and he gave me the lowdown on the house; and to sum it up, he basically said this: *Take it, keep its integrity, but make it yours.* And so began my love affair with the Laurel Canyon house.

Even though I had driven past that house for years, I really hadn't seen it. After Rick gave me the house, anyone who found out where I lived said: A) *I used to party in that house*; B) *I drive up and down Laurel Canyon all the time and have never seen it*; or C) *Isn't that Houdini's house that's haunted?*

When I first walked in the door to our new home, I may have cried. Just a little, and unfortunately, not with joy but with trepidation about what it was going to take to make this a family home. Our house was an untamed, beautiful beast, and I became determined to tame it but still respect the unique character and beautiful soul that was already there. I ended up becoming the designer and choosing an incredible architect, whose attitude and vibrancy was unmatched. We immediately clicked, and that's when I knew that this house, this beast, only needed some love, attention, and care to restore it to its former glory.

The staircase wasn't attached to the upstairs landing, the moldings were falling off the walls, and the carpet in the bedrooms, I found out, was originally tan. I knew that because when I lifted the mattress off the floor to throw it away, the carpet underneath was tan, in contrast to the stained dark brown it was everywhere else.

The systems in the house, all the things behind the walls that keep the house operating, i.e., heating and air, pipes, etc., were all older than me. Then we discovered there had been a fire in the house years before and some of the wood in the walls was burned. I cried again.

A family hadn't lived in the house, I don't think, ever. Yes, artists had lived there for periods of time, but I needed it turned into a family home. I had little kids, and animals, and I like heat! So, after wiping my tears, I summoned my knowhow from my upbringing, found a good contractor, and off I went.

This is my journey with my first home that would be featured in *Architectural Digest*.

We found a newspaper
from 1929 in the walls.
It just had layers of
character—it had a past.

Bringing together distinct pieces creates an eclectic yet cohesive family of design elements.

GUCCI MEETS GAP

I love walking into a store and getting that feeling in my bones that I'm going to find something great. An unusual piece or two that I'll fall in love with. The piece that speaks to me. You're probably picturing me in the vintage shops in Paris, London, or Italy, and that is very likely. But, it's just as likely that I'll find that piece in the ten-dollar shops in downtown Los Angeles, or driving through a small town.

If I had a house with all "precious" items (that's code for expensive), I would be worried all the time. Worried that something would be spilled on the fabric, or something would break. I never want to live that way. I want to enjoy every space—of course visually but also in comfortability.

I call it my Gucci meets Gap approach.

Let me explain.

My living room is where my kids have skateboarded, played tag, had parties, chased our dogs, our dogs chased them back, etc. All true.

I loved that that was happening in the house. I never shouted for them to stop. I shouted to tell them to go faster.

My living room is one of my happy places. What looks to be the most valuable could be from thrift shops, or something I stole from a family member's basement that they didn't care about anymore.

One of my favorite things in my living room is my white coffee table, where there are many small, Chinese vases resting on top. And I'll throw tall flowers in a few of the vases for even more of a statement. Looks like a million bucks, but between you and me, the most expensive vase is about ten dollars. So, a total of about $180. And yes, a vase was broken by a ball being thrown for Rufus, but it wasn't a big deal. I have reserves in one of my kitchen cabinets.

Now, I do have some lavish pieces. Pieces I've saved for! But I still want people to enjoy them. The high/low mix—the Gucci meets Gap—is my jam.

I call this my Sunday room.
Key ingredients: magazines,
newspaper, hot tea, quiet . . .

I don't want to create spaces that are too precious to be enjoyed. The whole point is that your home should make your life better.

My girls have a climbing wall in our house. They won't let me get rid of it even though they are bigger now. It brings them that joy.

Your personal space is a love letter to yourself. You can do what you want to do.

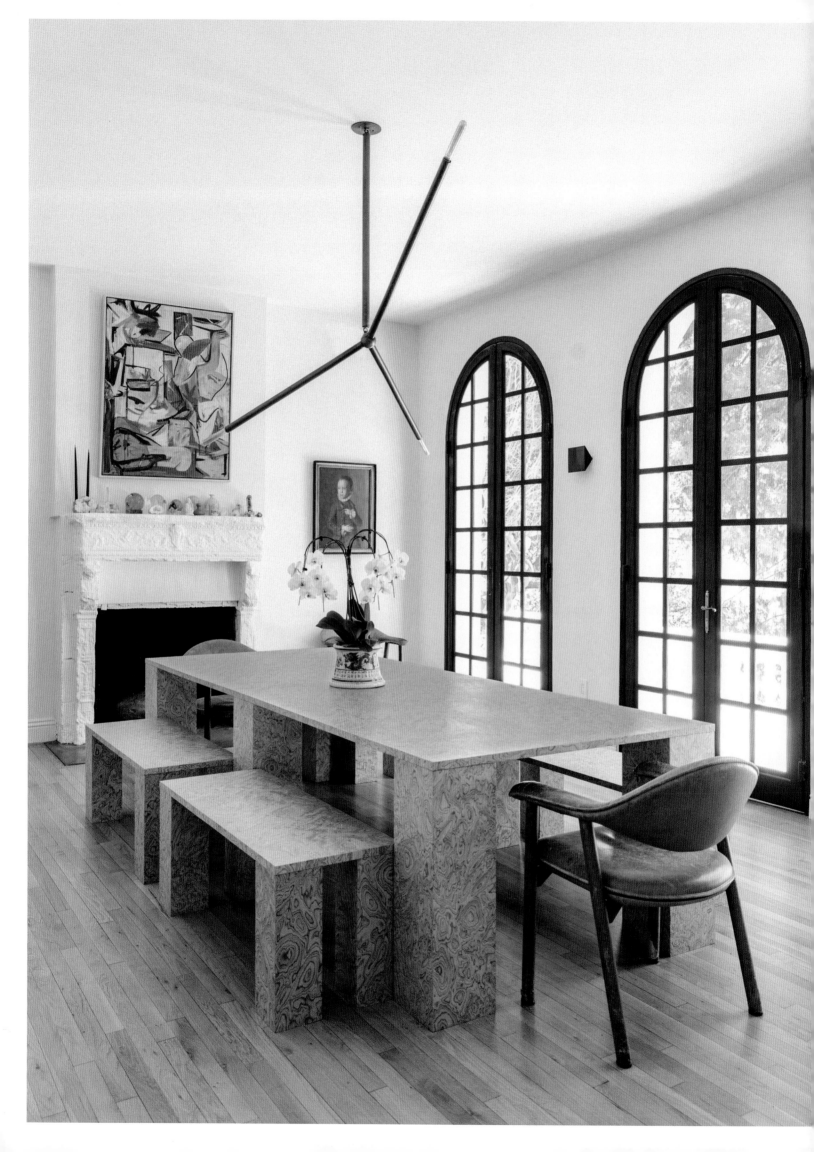

I ended up redoing the floors and making them lighter.

I can't help it. My need to experiment can make my family a bit crazy.

Text from Mark: "Hey, can you tell me where the sofa will be when I get home?"

That applied to furniture, lights, flooring. Like I said, I can't help it!

Starting with one piece is usually how it all comes together. So often what you see in my interiors are really strong pieces—they could be works of art or distinct pieces of furniture that I'm attracted to on their own and in combination with others. It's like creating a great meal by using different spices and ingredients to create and serve an exceptional feast.

7 A.M.

One morning, I got a call at about 7 a.m., and it was an unknown number. When I answered, I heard a familiar voice. She spoke fast and had the most infectious laugh—it was Molly Sims.

She had already been working with an incredible team but wanted fresh eyes on the project they'd all been designing for a while. So, I jumped right in and absolutely fell in love with the collaboration.

The home's design is clean and quite lovely—a modern twist on a classic, shingle-style home with a palette of white oak flowing throughout. What's nice about this project is that it's a striking environment and a well-thought-out building.

The design brief for the powder room was "Molly loves butterflies" and from there, I had free reign. I went to MJ Atelier, one of my favorites, and we designed the magical wallpaper for this space. Adding three-dimensional white butterflies and a few metallic ones made it feel surprising and so personal for Molly.

For the bar room, I focused on a design that was clean and minimal, keeping in line with the overall vibe of the house. The bar's fluting, stone, and brass touches are standouts while not being overwhelming. The inviting personality and glitz of this area make it feel like it's the company who are the stars in the room. Complete with Pierre Augustin Rose furniture, of course.

I'm all about feel, and this place has a fantastic feel to it from the moment you walk inside. It's important to me that my clients' spaces reflect who they are, and having been to Molly's home before, it's always buzzing. There's this lighthearted and luxury feel to it, and I wanted that connection, that feeling, to translate. The house radiates happiness—you feel welcomed and at ease, very much like its owner when you first meet or answer that early morning call.

Color affects us. Being intentional about the colors one chooses is important.

Do you have design rules you follow? Break them.

My ultimate goal is to please my clients in an unexpected way.

When my job is done, I want my client to be happy with the end result. It's about them.

A COLORFUL LIFE

This home in Los Feliz holds such a special place in my heart—it was one of the first homes I ever designed. It has such a rich history and elegant structure and it's easily one of the coolest houses.

The homeowners are a couple who are so full of joy and happiness. When I met them, it was evident that their family and friends were their core, and I wanted to embrace that throughout their home. With that in mind, the house is set up with conversation areas that bring in color.

The Spanish-style house had many details that had been preserved over the decades. I chose to highlight and accentuate what the space so beautifully already had to offer.

In the dining room, the blue walls embraced extraordinary artwork, and TG-10 Sling dining chairs, designed by William Katavolos, Ross Littell, and Douglas Kelley, flank the vintage dining table. The Ingo Maurer chandelier is its own art piece and is such a fun element in the space that allows for changing displays of personal drawings, notes, and other visuals.

With the living room, I wanted to celebrate the room's relationship with nature. That verdant green was just bursting with life and movement through the floor-to-ceiling windows. Using a custom blue that reflected the hue in the dining room, I created continuity in the house with a serene atmosphere replete with natural light. The vintage Hans Wegner Papa Bear armchairs provide an inviting focus for the cozy space, along with the gorgeous collection of personal items gathered from the couple's travels in the built-in bookcases.

In the bathroom, I decided to keep the original green tiles and patinaed mirror, bringing everything to life with the pink painted walls and a vintage crystal light over a modern, free-standing tub.

This client had decided to trade in the rush of LA to build the most serene escape in Malibu. He wanted a place for solitude as well as a home for game day with his boys.

With that information we knew we wanted the overall feeling to be inviting. We wanted to wrap the space in warmth and make it a clean through line. So the first thing we did was choose the wood that would wrap the floor all the way through the ceiling. The open concept and restrained color and materials palette created a visual connection from one space to another.

In the dining room, we kept it uncomplicated. The art brought in angular shapes that paired well with the diagonal of the Shou Sugi Ban staircase. We added vintage black leather dining chairs as a final touch. The contrasting colors contribute to the sense of calm, every item carefully selected for a laid-back feel.

The living area is unconventional, with a Ping-Pong table by James de Wulf front and center, along with cubist brass stools with sheepskin seat cushions that have a very sculptural feel. In the adjacent sitting room, contemporary, colorful art is juxtaposed against a striped vintage sofa, creating another unexpected combination of pieces.

The powder room is unexpected in the best way possible. We covered it from floor to ceiling with black-and-white cement tiles for a surprise. All the while, the primary bedroom bathroom is the opposite. It drips in tranquility and has all the vibe and energy of a spa. For fixtures, we wanted to create some whimsy, so we went with a pair of vintage sconces that we positioned to face different directions.

The owner had a vision for himself and his new family. He had put his heart and soul into his career, and now, creating this home, he truly wanted the ability to make it his ultimate refuge. He's since become a friend, and every time I go to visit I'm overwhelmed with joy for him, his family, and me, for getting to hang out there.

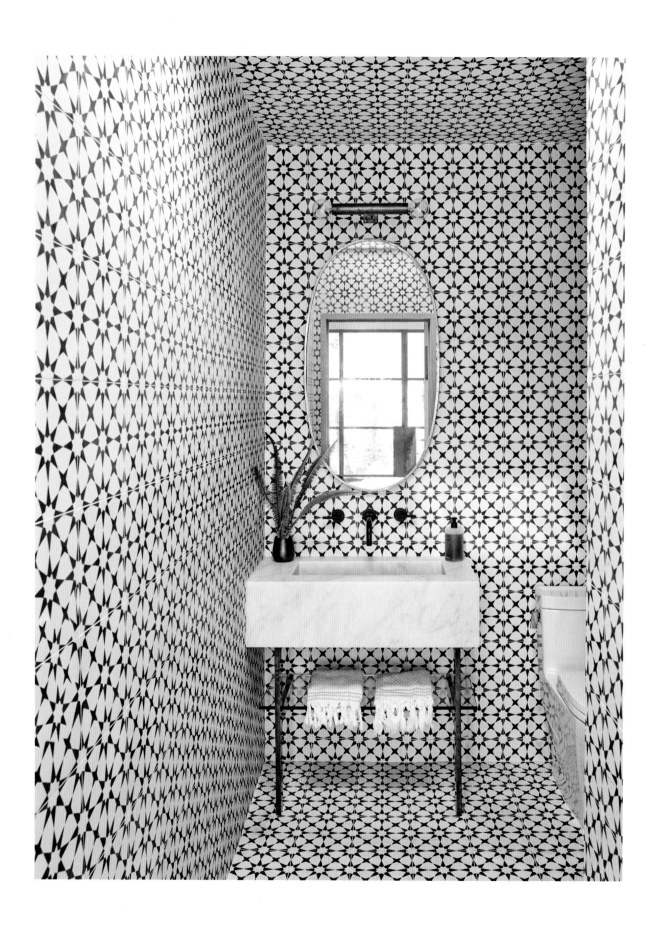

SIMPLY BEAUTIFUL

THIS. HOUSE. IS. INSANE. The good kind. The design is by modernist architect Ray Kappe, who is revered for his innovative way of engaging the outdoors and creating warmth through the extensive use of wood in his residences. Redwood, teak, and expansive glass are beautifully brought together in this stunning home.

This client had found me through a friend, and after a wonderful dinner with him and his fiancée talking about life, kids, design, and more, I knew we were kindred spirits. They were filled with such free-spirited energy and had a love of color and plants, much like myself!

For the family room, I wanted to respect the midcentury aesthetic of the space. I chose a Mah Jong modular sofa, made popular in the '70s, in a mix of patterns and colors that pick up both the warm tones of the wood and the blue of the swimming pool just outside the glass. This room has a boho vibe that is a layered and laid-back mix of textures. The round, stacked shapes on the coffee table and the additional curved chairs bring a softness to the rectilinear, architectural space.

For the beautiful, bright living room, I didn't need to do very much. The room, without one piece of furniture in it, was breathtaking. So, continuing to pay tribute to the surrounding greenery and architectural lines of the house, I found a pair of vintage chairs in a luscious Dedar textural fabric in rich browns, silvers, and golds. These chairs, against the curves of the vibrant, emerald-green Charles Zana mohair sofa, are beautiful. I didn't want to do anything heavy in the room, so I chose the Easca coffee table, made of melted down Irish crystal with marble legs (no two exactly the same). Then, to bring the funky, a black leather swing by Blackman Cruz.

In the dining room, I wanted a space where my client could enjoy good food and conversation. A space that was both relaxing but luxe. I broke up the straight lines of the space by bringing in curvilinear chairs. I used a wild, plush, velvet fabric that sings. I love the way the colors come together in this room, embodying the dynamics of the home's exterior. It's important in a space that nothing competes but instead is harmonious with the other elements. Being able to create that duality through lines and shapes creates a lovely language and energy in a house, one surrounded with such overwhelming beauty, so that it still maintains comfort and warmth.

Completing the space is the bedroom. I was lucky to find the bed frame and side tables, designed by Paul Evans, all in excellent condition. The pieces reflect the light and greenery of the outdoor environment inside. The subtle wallpaper of the space echoes the rectangular shapes of the furniture, providing a neutral backdrop for the gorgeous, framed Hermès scarf (the clients own and part of the inspiration), and the soft Pierre Augustin Rose sofa facing the outdoors. A custom sheepskin rug pulls everything together, creating, again, that duality between shapes.

In a simple, clean space, it needs to be all about the details—this hand-crafted table is a simple detail that I truly love. The shape, the legs, the organic top made from melted Irish crystal—a work of art.

For the dining room, I wanted to bring in curvilinear forms with the table and chairs, as well as a relaxed vibe, so that you're supported and can enjoy the space for many hours.

I used a wild, lush, velvet fabric on the chairs that complements the lines of the table. I love the way the colors come together and embody everything dynamic happening outside.

Making sure nothing competes but instead is harmonious is so important because it creates a through line and a really lovely language and energy in the house, surrounded by all this overwhelming beauty while maintaining comfort and warmth.

GOLDEN SUNSET

I was incredibly honored to be approached by Piaget to design their Rodeo Drive store. They only asked that I follow the company's timeless and iconic reputation, and that the store give a nod to California, Hollywood specifically.

California sunsets are absolutely breathtaking. I decided to pull from the colors of the sky, sand, and ocean waters. It was an incredible journey to find the synergy here, going with a mix of vintage, custom, and new designs, and the DNA of the brand, which of course is most important.

The brass details throughout the entire space complement the natural tones of the furniture and custom silk wallpapers, providing an appealing contrast that further highlights the jewelry and watches on display.

Against such exquisite items, I had the opportunity to bring in a little bit of whimsy. I designed a bold, custom carpet in the seating area inspired by their jewelry. It echoes other curvilinear elements in the store, and the navy blue provides an accent of color amidst the otherwise neutral aesthetic. The midcentury modern "Cubo" sofa by Brazilian designer Jorge Zalszupin was sightly reworked to make it commercially viable, and to stand up to the wear and tear of everyday foot traffic, while maintaining the original design.

The aim was to make every inch of the store beautiful, so that when the eye takes in the full store, nothing is out of place. On the men's side, the blue lacquer is a tribute to the luxury watches, creating a dynamic sense of strength. The gold wallpaper on the women's side is luxe and looks beautiful against any woman's complexion.

The end result is an elegant jewelry box of a space that is a nod to classic Hollywood while celebrating the unmistakable sophistication and quality of the Piaget brand.

I decided to pull from the colors of the sky, sand, and ocean waters. It was an incredible journey to find the synergy here, going with a mix of vintage, custom, and new designs.

AN OLDIE BUT A GOODIE

An historic home, built in the 1920s, the Isle house has many rich details that were immediately intriguing. It was a lovely challenge to honor those aspects while also creating a new space for the owners. I wanted to celebrate the crown moldings, French windows, and other original trim, whether large or small, that would contribute to the overall sense of grandeur.

The fun part was to disrupt the expectation of those specific details, to turn it on its head by adding to the vibe with new pieces and makers.

These clients have two children, and they wanted pieces that could be functional and sturdy without sacrificing style. Using a simple palette created the desired feel throughout the home, and the color change in the bedroom brought a sense of drama, as well as privacy and intimacy.

In the living room, layered area rugs created texture and a sense of flair, with a collection of vintage and contemporary furniture in two separate seating areas for entertaining or everyday life.

Iconic Franco Albini armchairs by Poggi Pavia in the family room may have scared off other clients with children, but they actually are extremely functional, with plenty of potential to hide errant spills and crumbs.

I used a Venetian plaster finish on the powder room walls that has a nice sheen to it while remaining restrained. Washed in pretty light and with this quality of plastering, the nuances are really beautifully revealed. I wanted the wall color to be dark specifically because I wanted it to create a cavernous mood and feeling. It sets the backdrop for the clients' collection of really cool moments in there. With crystals, contemporary Apparatus lighting, and Charlotte Perriand sconces, it's almost as if you've discovered a little, secret room with sweet, personal objects. And that's what a powder room is. It's a little jewel box to do whatever you want with, and that's what I love about it.

The den's original wood-paneled walls are illuminated by a wonderful Noguchi Akari light, in the largest size possible, hung ridiculously low! Though it in no way impedes movement in the room while casting such a beautiful glow. A cozy, enveloping room. Chess, anyone?

This breakfast nook is a mix of unique pieces in a small space that lead to such a beautiful, outside area. The light from the double glass doors pours into the room and glints off the sculptural Paul Matter light fixture in swirling brass. That is such a fun, genius piece.

Distinct pieces can come together without fighting but rather blend and enhance one another as if they're two different personalities in conversation. The curvy Roly Poly chair, designed by Faye Toogood, and the boxy vintage wood chair make an unlikely, happy couple and make this such a sweet spot. When all was said and done, this simple room became one of my favorites.

SHE SAID YES!

I had worked with this couple before—they were my very first clients. They asked me for help after seeing my home, and I was so grateful for their trust in me. Fourth street was our third project together, their new home. We searched for a couple of years, and it was like dating. We saw a lot of NO's, a couple of maybes and finally a YES! She said yes! And she was right. Waiting for the right fit is very important!

This house is light and airy. It has such a lovely feeling to it. The home is a traditional Hamptons style, with shingles, greenery, and large, wonderful windows.

In the dining room, the pink and teal colors felt chic and playful. The space is adorned with knock-out art pieces, a glossy red apple and a piece by Richard Prince from his Instagram series that features Candice Swanepoel's matching ruby lips. Across from the French doors, is a Jake Longstreth painting that fit so well with the existing palette that it instantly worked well in the space. With so much brilliant color, to complete the space, I went with a natural hue for the dining table that is a vintage-inspired design by Rose Uniacke—keeping the room bright and balanced.

In the breakfast nook, a vintage table and chairs soaks up the natural light—it was a set I had difficulty parting with because I was so in love with it myself. There was a brief moment when I may have considered keeping these pieces for myself, but I couldn't imagine a better home for them.

These clients are some of the most giving and welcoming people I know. Their door is always open to their friends, day or night. I've tested this myself! They are the definition of livable luxe. A movie producer, always looking at the practical side of things: Are the measurements correct? Will my friends be comfortable sitting here for hours? Is the fabric durable? His wife, the most stylish, always wanting to know the look, the colors, the feel, and of course, will it be gorgeous when it's done? This project became the perfect intersection of beauty and function.

I'm no art critic, not an authority in any way. I simply know what I like and respond to. And honestly, that's all you have to know.

Sometimes, art is the star in the room, and sometimes it's a quiet conversation piece.

CREATIVE CULTURE

These clients are super cool, a family of artists in their respective careers, and flat-out art lovers. I love having meetings with them because they'll share a new art piece, or a recent gallery visit. And that was the design brief, let the art, a painting, sculpture or furniture, be the star. The project didn't need many pieces, just a clear direction and point of view.

The dining room is minimalist but has all it requires. The Pierre Jeanneret table and chairs are pieces of art unto themselves. Vintage, octagonal floor tiles also provide a pop of color and contrast against the walls, framing the dining set beautifully. To balance the lines of the furniture, the curves of the Murano chandelier—a lovely statement piece on its own— brought softness and elegance. Having so few pieces in the space was intentional, and I think the end result is really quite spectacular. I can be minimalist, or a maximalist, I love all of it. This one in particular is a lesson in understated beauty and sophistication. Likewise, the hallway is like a gallery space that displays several unique works of art including a Haas Brothers bench that provides whimsy and a sense of motion.

The Rick Owens daybed in the living room is a spectacular piece, not only to look at but to lay on . . . enjoy. Stunning Ferrari Sheppard artworks frame the window in an embrace, providing a fluidity of color that flows from the swimming pool outside to the complementary rug within. That's where you get into design being in the details. It's just a few pieces, but they all connect in such a beautiful, seamless way. As avid art collectors, the homeowners appreciated these details as well.

Designed with input from the homeowners' children, the bathrooms are a departure from the rest of the house, and the result is so sweet. A bit of inspiration came from the Chateau Marmont, a Los Angeles institution, for their daughter's bathroom, using floor tiles with delicate flowers and embracing her favorite color, pink, which I adore of course. For their little boy, I wanted something graphic. The combination of tiles is sophisticated, but still subtle. I love the way the bathrooms came together and brought out the personalities of the children, which was most important. It's an excellent representation of the ability to show that bathrooms can truly be personal, one's own statement.

One of my favorite moments in the house is the pink tile I used in the pool. I usually get requests for blues and greens, which I love to use, but this pink was a refreshing take on pool tiles, that glimmer so beautifully in the sunlight.

WHERE MY GIRLS AT?

These ladies are my girls, my crew! I was instantly drawn to their elegance and worldliness.

They purchased this New York City apartment in a pre-war art deco building and were working with the world renowned architect, Richard Gluckman. Having worked with these ladies before, Richard was able to articulate what he knew to be important to them, and he and I couldn't have gotten along better.

In the entryway I used these beautiful sconces the couple already owned. I paired them with deep-blue, Venetian-plastered walls, which contrast so nicely with the original steel front door. This entry area is its own moment that prepares you for the apartment itself—with its mix of styles and eras. When you move from the entrance into the living room, the shift is dramatic, and I love the relationship between the hues from one space to the next.

The sitting room is its own bold color story in shades of blue that augment the owner's incredible photography. I recovered the existing closet doors in this dimensional, patterned velvet fabric that allows you to discover something new each time you look. I brought in other jewel tone velvets that are used on the sofa and vintage chairs. The brass ceiling light is the jewelry that was added to bring the shine and connect with all the other color. This room is an area to converse, or pick a book from the shelves that house some of their favorite authors.

The powder room provides a quick moment to do something great and dramatic in a small space. The grid of the blue repeating tile provides a background and contrast to the playful, hand-made round mirror with tiled-in floral elements, as well as a cylindrical sink. The color of the space also ties back to the front entry.

The living room is all about pinks and grays. The Vladimir Kagan sofa is just spectacular—the shape of it was perfect for this apartment—it adds definition and dimension to the room. The Pucci chair is all about turning the otherwise sophisticated aesthetic on its head, throwing in some playfulness. It's the exclamation mark at the end of the sentence!

Color can really dictate
the mood of a room; it can
create a great statement.

SHAKEN NOT STIRRED

This house is located in the Trousdale neighborhood of Los Angeles. It's one of my favorite areas—the history, the houses, the streets. The likes of Elvis Presley, Frank Sinatra, Dean Martin, and Ray Charles (among many other notable names) have called Trousdale home, situated in the foothills of the Santa Monica mountains. The residential area was developed in the 1950s and '60s by Paul Trousdale, and architects such as Frank Lloyd Wright, A. Quincy Jones, and Paul R. Williams lent their skills to some of the neighborhood's mid-century modernist homes.

In the past four years, this is my fifth project with this client. I love it! For a designer, a repeat client is the best feeling, because they really believe that you get them, you understand how they live and what's important to them. He has such a beautiful way of thinking about things that's consistently positive, constantly looking for the good in any given situation. It's truly inspiring, and I wanted that reflected in the house. He's a man of few words, and those words I needed to take in to understand his vision. After some time, however, I realized that he only speaks a few words because he focuses on the key elements I need to know—from there he trusts me to bring the concept to life on his and his husband's behalf.

The colors I chose are a reflection of his wonderful energy. The dining room features a custom-made stone table, echoing the original design of the terrazzo floor, that I framed with pink carpet. The colors complement both the striking painting by Collins Obijaku as well as the LA landscape just outside the window. It also features a pendant light by Bec Brittain called the Echo, a pair of vintage sconces, and the Mario Bellini dining chairs.

In the living room I designed a custom curved sofa that hugs the original wooden screen. The petal-shaped light fixture and bold yellow armchairs echo the colors in the painting in the dining room. This is a house to gather in, drink martinis, and to share fun stories.

THE GREATS OF THE GREAT

I love the ladies of the Great—they are so gracious and kind and have become my sisters. I really respect what they've built and how they've done it while remaining best friends and business partners for years.

When working with a brand, it's important to immerse yourself in that brand's culture to understand what's important to them. With a home, you're focused on creating this warm, cozy, inviting place, but to work in a commercial environment, there are additional factors to consider and restrictions to adhere to while still creating something beautiful.

Emily and Merritt truly care about every single detail, and every aspect of their business is considered and put together with intention, down to the striped curtain of the dressing room. These ladies are passionate about what they do, and that has an effect on me in every meeting. It only makes me want to do better. In designing with them for the past few years, some of the pieces have become staples in each store. That makes my heart swell, in knowing that I really get what they care about.

Their clothing, like them, is effortless elegance. So my internal design brief was to make the stores extensions of who they are. The color of the walls are interpretations of their clothing—an army jacket or a vintage denim. At this point, we've designed multiple stores together, and it's still new every time. There are certain items that are staples, but it's a new experience each time. I only wish they could open another fifty stores!

It begins with a conversation about textures and colors, and finding the harmony between the two.

The pieces you choose need to create no conflict with each other, to flow. You can do this by looking at the space between them and the shapes in the air around each element.

By introducing gentle curves that complement each other, and spacing them apart so their outlines have room to breathe, it will all come together.

FOR THE LOVE OF ART

The house was last touched by the remarkable designer, Jane Hallworth. We had big shoes to fill. Gulp. So many great things had been done, and our job was to add to the vibe. It has been years since Jane completed the project, but she's such an icon in design, and we were honored to work where she had worked.

The living room is a relaxing space with ample seating, a salon for great conversation and striking works of art. Even the tree has a visual relationship to the large-scale paintings and sculptures adorning the room.

The dramatic light fixture and the stunning metallic fireplace already existed when we came in, so it was about finding everything else to complement those aspects in the living room. The three vintage chairs are completely unique from one another but get along beautifully as one eclectic family. The rug unifies all the different elements, including the color of the wood beams, the furniture, the art, and even the tree. Passion and love for this space ultimately produced the desired results. There was lovely materiality, warm colors, and a lot of softness—it's just easy but really directional as well. You can be in this room for hours and hours, which I really love.

In the bedroom, pink walls highlight the vintage brown leather De Sede sofa with a multi-hued photography installation. The art brought the color, and guess who brought the pink? It allowed the art to be front and center and made it even more vibrant.

Grouping together the Eero Saarinen Egg chair and Isamu Noguchi Akari floor lamp set against the lush, green oil painting by Wilfried Prager created a standout moment. I love a moment, a vignette. These clients do as well. Their environment needed to be as interesting as they are. The result is a distinct and original vibe.

I start by taking three items at a time—just three—and playing with those and moving them around, maybe changing them out, replacing them. I do it again and again until it's right.

VISTA VIEWS

These clients are a wonderful couple, with three beautiful daughters. The house has walls of glass that open to the yard and the incredible view of Los Angeles beyond. My design brief was making sure nothing was too harsh or bright and didn't stop your eye from going straight to that view. I wanted to bring in great shapes with the furniture pieces, no loud colors or patterns.

The main room is a big, open space, where the dining room, kitchen, and living room all blend seamlessly. I wanted the fabric of the couch to complement the kitchen marble, and that marble to match with the living room colors. All one big happy family, like my clients. I also went with coziness all the way without sacrificing style.

In the family room, I designed the travertine wall and fireplace where a blank white wall previously stood. The coffee table was a vintage piece that I found that I became obsessed with—a beautiful piece where a furniture designer was thinking out of the box—and it fit perfectly in front of the classic Hans Wegner Papa Bear chair in a gray fabric. It's a model example of the balance of new and old coming together to produce something pleasing and timeless.

Likewise, what was once a storage closet, is now an exceptional den. As the rest of the house is so open, it was nice to make a space that was a reveal. When the custom wood door is closed, you don't know there's a room behind it. I designed the custom wood slatted walls that were produced offsite and then meticulously installed. I paired the classic De Sede DS 600 sofa—in a beat-up (just enough) leather—with the Serge Mouille pendant light and Roger Capron coffee table. All of these exquisite, vintage pieces are offset by the contemporary black silk rug, wood wall enclosure, and the custom-made stone bar.

My favorite approach to design is eclecticism. If you can find different pieces that sit harmoniously together, the end result will last for years and years.

Blush-colored plaster, onyx sconces, and fluted wood all work together to make this a calm and pretty space. I try to bring these small moments of beauty in my interiors that can really influence a person's mood.

TREE-LINED STREET

I have loved this neighborhood of Los Angeles for as long as I can remember. Extra-wide streets filled with the most beautiful enormous trees, where it always feels like a fall day, and the houses are grand. Working on one of these gorgeous homes in my favorite area made me feel I was experiencing a full-circle moment. Lucky girl.

The clients are absolutely lovely. They had found their dream home, a 1920s Spanish house with high ceilings and tall walls. Their vision for their home needed to be an extension of them: beautiful, colorful, and classic.

The living room was kept white to lean into the breathtaking height of the room. The color and the grounding of the room comes in with the pieces of furniture, the sky blue marble console tables, the rose-colored chairs, and the graphic rug and artwork.

In the dining room, I went with a dark, rich blue and brought in furniture pieces that popped. I focused on silver and brass as material choices, and the chairs upholstered in a gorgeous, deep blue velvet.

For the family room, I wanted to create a space that felt welcoming, tucked away from the openness of the house—a spot where you could share secrets and have great conversations and family time. I found a couple of the iconic Gerard van den Berg Rock chairs. I think I searched the globe until I found a total of four. I recovered the set while maintaining their integrity, and they absolutely make this space. These rare vintage chairs and stunning artwork, are paired with the bronze coffee table by Philip and Kelvin LaVerne. The light above is a vintage, Italian piece, which focuses on the table, creating a beautiful glow and an inviting environment. When the room is not in use with the kids, the adults can use it as a drinks-before-dinner space, an extension of the adjacent dining room. There is a soulfulness and sense of comfort throughout the entire home, but this area is a favorite.

I found a couple of the iconic Gerard van den Berg Rock chairs. I think I searched the globe until I found a total of four. I recovered the set while maintaining their integrity, and they absolutely make this space.

CHALET FOR THE DAY

This stunner of a house feels like it could be in a European ski town. A chalet. So, the fact that it's in the states and is a new build, with that aesthetic, was like heaven to work on. It was so beautifully done.

This deliberately aged space is breathtaking. With the finish on the wood panels, it definitely feels as if it's been there for a hundred years, an unusual room for California which makes it so special. The ceiling light fixture by David Wiseman makes the space feel like a fairytale.

The coffee table, blue sofa, and floor cushions are vintage, whereas the striking black chairs—while clearly vintage inspired—are actually brand new by Roman and Williams. I love the profile.

The adjoining spaces also combine an eclectic selection of pieces. The Studio Giancarlo Valle sofa is such an elegant combination of wood and upholstery and has such a lovely sculptural quality to it. The curves beautifully echo the railing of the staircase. The Flag Halyard chair by Hans Wegner is another statement piece that is light and linear and contrasts so superbly with the chunky sofa.

In theory, if you put all this on paper, it shouldn't work, but when you put it together in the space, it just clicks.

7172

lly Postcards

Jasper Johns: Mind/Mirror

Martin Puryear Liberty Libertà

REIGNING SUPREME

This house sits on a stunning street with a commanding presence. Grand Craftsmans sit next to Tudors and Spanish-style homes—a collection of 1920s gems. This home is one of them. Tudor details such as the pointed arch doors and the original patina on the brick are standout features.

This couple knows their stuff. They are involved in the local community, sit on the board of museums, and are just cool folk. They are a vibrant family and I wanted that vibrancy reflected in the interiors. It's a joy to exchange stories and ideas with these clients. They care so much about each piece and its origins.

In the living room, their brief to me was open ended. They wanted to allow the process to unfold naturally. The only thing was to keep the piano for family concerts.

The coffee table was the starting point for the room, and it's an exquisite one, a limited edition art piece by David/Nicolas—one in a series of eight made of travertino bronzo and stainless steel. Being shipped from Europe, this beauty had quite the journey. I had fallen in love with it from afar and showed it to the homeowners, and they were onboard. Even though it took eight men and three hours to install it, we wouldn't change a thing. It is an art piece unto itself.

This house is filled with contemporary artists, so the colors I chose were selected with their artwork in mind. Even the shapes of the curved Pierre Augustin Rose sofas that face each other in the living room make it so you can view and appreciate the art.

I covered the PAR sofas in a celadon mohair. Ahhhh, so pretty. I love the pale green with the yellow dress from the painting by Calida Rawles.

Four Zanuso chairs reupholstered in a cream velvet and a contemporary metal table create a lovely conversation corner, in what was previously a forgotten little space. The bold, colorful painting by Amoako Boafo sets the mood. This spot is where they could spend time talking with friends and sharing their musings on art.

With this home I wanted to create a beautiful story, so all the pieces have a history. Rather than strictly evaluating items for their instant aesthetic appeal, I appreciated the investment the homeowners had—they were interested to know everything from who made it to the story behind it, far beyond whether they found it pretty or not. It was extremely fun to work with them because I grew as a designer, and we all loved the end result.

BEAUTY IS AS BEAUTY DOES

WHAT'S IN THE INSIDE FLOWS TO THE OUTSIDE

I've been thinking about how to even begin this. Talking about Gwyneth makes my heart full. Truly.

Someone once said to me, "You get why some people are mega humans." She is one. It's not because she's famous, or ridiculously beautiful, or funny as all get out. But because, without knowing it, she walks into a room and makes it better. Her kindness, energy, willingness to just give of herself without a second thought, her honesty, and support for her friends. Yeah, she's a mega human—one I've been fortunate to know for more than twenty years.

When Gwyneth hired me, I knew she had worked with some really talented designers, so she'd expect a lot from me. And even though my firm was only two years old at that point, she didn't doubt me for a second. She believed in me more than I did. Insanely kind, ain't it?

I knew she'd seen lots of good furniture pieces, and she loves design. So, I was going to have to push myself to show her items she hadn't seen before and really wow her. And even though I went to our design meeting shaking in my boots, I left feeling like I'd grown as a person, and a designer.

Thanks, sis.

The design brief was the home they would retire to, their exhale place. Spending holidays and weekends there. Always filled with family and friends. And it had to be unique and pretty, layered with calming colors, luscious materials and striking pieces. But still with a bit of playfulness. A backdrop to her life.

Her view is spectacular—you just can't compete with it. So, I pulled colors from the outside and brought them inside: pale greens, browns, creams, golds, and tans. The living room is a tour de force of singular pieces like the oversized luxe Jim Zivic hammock, the Rick Owens chair, signature artwork by John Baldessari, Ed Ruscha, and D'lisa Creager, and the most playful and elegant light sculpture by Lindsey Adelman that dances across the ceiling.

The house silently screams beauty. I gave it everything I had—it's a stunner, and she's happy. That's all I care about.

Design is the alchemy of
so many different elements
coming together.

A scenic, pastoral wallpaper wraps around the dining room and feels like a dreamy interpretation of the landscape just outside the floor-to-ceiling glass doors.

I believe with all my heart that we're enhanced by our surroundings, and if I can bring beauty into people's lives, then that creates good feelings.

Powder rooms should
be about expecting . . .
the unexpected.

MY SAFE SPACE

I really didn't realize I was looking for a new space. My old office was perfectly lovely. But late one night I was looking at spaces online (forever a design junkie)—and this space looked intriguing. There was a picture of this long corridor and then a huge, white box with high ceilings and wood beams. That's when I knew this was going to be Romanek Design Studio.

Everything just kept clicking. When I first toured the space, I saw immediately what it should be. What I needed it to be. The design brief I created for myself was serenity, a soft palette, and just a few key statement pieces. So, I added skylights between the bow trusses and desks with divider walls that are a minimalist moment all covered in celadon paint. It's a place where the team can have their own distinct spaces and yet turn to each other to collaborate. The library hang spot is for everyone to enjoy and utilize.

The bulk of the office is plants. Just plants. And the result is joyous for us. A palette cleanser after too much stimulation. When clients come by for the first time, they always appreciate the vibe. The office serves as a living, breathing example of what we can do for our clients and how we can address their individual needs. For us, this is a workspace, but also an oasis. A really happy, beautiful one.

Moment is a powerful word. It's used to help express an emotion.

That was a moment I'll never forget.

That was the moment that changed everything.

Design has moments too. When you look around the room, something strikes you more than anything else, causing you to stop and look again—maybe one piece, or a vignette.

These photos are a curation
of moments that have meant
so much to me.

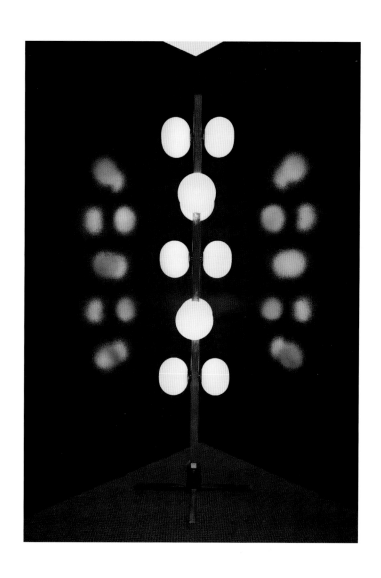

If you'd have asked me, even a year ago, if I'd ever
have a book, I would have said, not a chance.

I've learned with looking at these photos that I love a
good chaise, a fun color choice, art, and my clients.
Thank you to each of you for the trust you've shown me,
and the creative outlet you provided for me and my soul.

My aunts, uncles, and cousins, thank you so
much for your love and support for me and Mom.
Love you so much!

Thank you, thank you to Mayer Rus and Amy Astley
for seeing me before I did.

Estee Stanley for working together on The Bu and
East Channel Road, and for all the laughs.

Alix Frank and the entire DBA team.
Gloria and Steve from Chronicle Chroma, for listening
to me and schooling me along the way.

To the photographers who showed me another
way to see the spaces, I'm grateful to you!
Thank you so very much.

To Michael Clifford, wow, wow, wow, your photography
is truly stunning, but more importantly your heart is
kind and I look forward to working with you every time.
Wow wow wow.

Ana, Blanca, and my Jess.

And the RDS team, whom I couldn't do this without.

Of course, Mark R.

CREDITS

Livable Luxe by Brigette Romanek
Foreword by Gwyneth Paltrow

Publisher: Gloria Fowler, Steve Crist
Art Director and Editor: Gloria Fowler
Designer and Production: Alexandria Martinez
Production: Freesia Blizard
Copy Editor: Sara DeGonia
Pre-Press: John Bailey

ISBN: 978-1-7972-2400-8

Library of Congress Cataloging-in-Publication Data available.

Manufactured in China

Chronicle Chroma

Chronicle Chroma is an imprint of Chronicle Books
Los Angeles, California

chroniclechroma.com